Differen. .... Same Coin

A Collection of Poems

by

Chyrel J. Jackson

And

Lyris D. Wallace

Black Expression

Volumes I & II

Black Expression

Volume I

The Words Poured Out

I Know I Been Changed...

Chyrel J. Jackson

ISBN 9781723998348 (Paperback Edition)
Library of Congress Control Number:TXu2-149-932

Editing by: Jasmyne Deitzler and Cam Johns
Book Interior Design by: Usman Monday
Ebook Cover Designer: Jasmine C. Robinson

Printed and bound in the United States of America.

Published by Kindle Direct Publishing
P.O. Box 81226
Seattle, WA 98108 US
https://kdp.amazon.com

Dedication

This one's for my parents: Edna Mae, Wallace

Sylvester S. Wallace,

& My Beloved Micheal

One lifetime in your presence just isn't enough!

Acknowledgements

My parents, Edna Mae & Sylvester S. Wallace. My happiest memories: the music, enumerable books, and an extraordinary family. Dad, thank you for teaching us to have tenacity. I now understand you. Every day the Lord allows me to see I'll walk into it in your words, *"giving em' hell."*

Micheal, you have taught me the most about love's value. What it is, isn't, and patience. Seems like yesterday that we were taking our vows. I can now finally exhale. You are my forever love.

I have an amazing family. I will always treasure every moment spent with you. Thanks for inspiring all of the words.

Felicia, Antoine, Lauren, India, Jasmine, and Jonah (Ezra).

Lyris, I couldn't imagine taking this journey with anyone other than you. I literally used you as my pillow as we were but cradled babies. You are literally, the other half of myself-Smile.

Extended family Mama Elizabeth, (Mom) Barbara, (Mom) Muriel, Jozie Maxine, Bella, Jennifer, and the Glam Squad: Isaiah, Joy, & Faith.

The Brantley family: I couldn't ask for better friends. You were there when the bottom fell out. I'll love you always. Thank you.

Almost last, but certainly not least, to all my Rust College kids, you are the lifeline of what makes learning vital. You have given me many happy memories and even more reason to smile. Great Thanks, I love you all.

Thanks to every person that has been part of our lives and celebrate this work with us especially our readers.

Special Thanks and acknowledgement to the Great I am unto all generations, who created language that makes the words possible. Thank you!

Table of Contents

"Round-faced Girl"
(Lyris' Poem II)

I hear you talkin', round-faced girl.

    Speaking loud and clear.

Eyes like mine,

    Speech like mine,

        I can't believe it.

Teeth like mine,

    funk like mine,

        cool like mine.

Even got a jazzy, bluesy, soul like mine.

    Lyrically correct with perfect rhyme.

I hear you talkin', round-faced girl.

    Speaking loud and clear.

        Tone like mine,

          sound like mine,

style like mine.

Even got a sassy, mellow, flow like mine.

Lyrically correct with perfect rhyme.

I hear you talkin', round-faced girl.

Speaking loud and clear.

Eyes like mine,

Speech like mine;

I can't believe it.

Teeth like mine

Lyrically correct with perfect rhyme.

cjj '99

We Are One

All God's Chillung Got Wings...

"Greatness"
(Ezra's Declaration I)

As the years go by, I remember every second

    you were born.

I want to etch every unique line of your

    face upon the memory of my heart.

I remember a tiny, little baby boy with

    bright, curious, shiny, eyes.

The years have gone by as I recall the

    brilliance of your smile.

You are growing up and the world is

    yours to conquer.

You are my happiest memory.

    I was captured by your miraculous presence

as you were pulled from my sister's womb.

    17 years later and I am still annexed by

every breathing, moment of you.

You are all that is perfect and right in the
world. I see the hope of all that is possible, and the
expectation of what you could be radiates
within my soul.

Conquer the haters and naysayers, Ezra.
They never mattered anyway.

You were born to do big things.
That is what I see whenever I am in your divine
space.
Never give in to self-doubt. Rise above your
Challenging circumstances.
When you arrive at the difficult part of life and
you most certainly will, remember that your
molecular structure was and always will be
greatness.
That is what and who you are;
GREAT.
Go out into the world, young man. Unafraid

to expel your divine nature.

It is yours to conquer.

Your future shines brighter than the sun.

There is nothing greater than YOU...

cjj '18

"My Heart is Happiest
Watching Ezra Dance"

A carefree, teenaged black boy

    dances the night away

in his mother's love-filled kitchen.

    Happy hands and feet

wave and glide soulfully across

    the checkered tiled floor.

How monumental this moment.

    Watching a black boy safe

at home tonight, from the

    rage-filled world outside,

that won't allow teenaged black

    boys to blissfully dance.

                   cjj '18

"Moonchild"
(Lyris' Poem I)

Hello, round-faced girl with the prickly hair.

You are my greatest joy.

When I think of you, a thousand perfectly shaped
moons come to mind.

I am recalling your smile;

Lighting up my life, just like the moon illuminates
a dark and somber sky.

You're a very old soul. Your wisdom far exceeds
your years.

Tell me, have you been here before?

We are extended selves sharing in joy, feeling each
other's pain.

You are my heart's delight.

You are one perfectly shaped moon illuminating
my life.

cjj '97

Another Part of Me

Come Down Angels...

"Refined Jewels"
Life Lessons from Dad (Dad's Poem II)

We spend so much of our lives

running away from

fighting with and against

who and what we are.

Afraid of just being.

Frightened of what is true.

Truth and acceptance are life's

greatest gifts.

Usually only garnered through

the furnace of our affliction.

These refined jewels of life can

only be fully appreciated

with age.

Within the finite passage

of time acceptance is learned.

In all of life's combat

we find ourselves.

Once all the hurtful words are exchanged,

and all our unhealed pain
acknowledged,

we stand-firmly,

rooted in our truth.

Choosing whether to be broken or not.

cjj '18

"Mangoes & Sunshine"
(Dad's Poem I)

Love is my father bringing

    me mangoes on

lazy, hot, summer afternoons.

    Telling me stories, that make me laugh

and listening to me read poetry.

    which to him, doesn't always make

sense.

    Love is watching a smile form on his face,

causing me to think of a million rays of

    sunshine dancing across very

blue skies.

    He has such a nice smile,

when he chooses to smile.

    Love is laughing at my father's

old stories and jokes even though their meaning

sometimes escapes me.

Love is spending time with my

father, eating mangoes, on

lazy, hot, summer afternoons.

cjj '97

"Boxing the Wind"
(Felicia's Declaration II)

The world was your oyster. You were our

  beginning.

You always went your own way,

  sailing through life; opinions be damned.

You had to do it your way.

  I don't know where your Rudder

veered off course.

  I've watched your navigation instrument,

your compass, vacillate between the absurd and

  bizarre for most of my life.

You were blessed with beauty and talent, yet

  Never knew you possessed such gifts.

You always seem to be boxing the wind in a

  Category 5 Hurricane.

Self-doubt and fear have held you back for way

too long. If only you knew you have so
much to offer.

The kindness of our mother flows through
your veins.

Sylvester's confidence was the genetic
master design of your spectacular molecular

structure.

"Get it together, girl." Shake off the self-loathing,

and shame of past mistakes. Leave them
behind you.

You're in a race of one. Be your best self.
Achieve

your own greatness. It's in you to do so.
I always knew you could succeed in life. It is as

much of your DNA as chromosomes,
molecules and blood type.

Put away your boxing gloves, Laila. Stop fighting yourself.

The only person stopping you from greatness is YOU.

We are Edna Mae's girls and that, dear sister, is our majestic blue-print of

unparalleled purpose.

cjj '18

"Bright Yellow Banana Peels"
(Felicia's Poem I)

Sisters are people who wear your

    clothes without your permission.

They borrow earrings and make-up

    and conveniently forget to

bring them back.

Sisters are mirror images of self,

    who fight, laugh, cry and

gossip on the phone.

Sometimes older Sisters give younger Sisters

    Bus fare to further their education

and simply, get to work.

Sometimes Sisters frustrate you beyond

    human reason.

But mostly, you accept and love them because,

more than defining who

you are,

Sisters are ultimately You.

cjj '97

"Southpaw Contender"
(Felicia's Poem II)

You have ducked, dodged and taken

    many hits.

Life has had you against the ropes

    more times than I can count.

You just keep on swingin'.

    Boxing the wind,

        Boxing the wind

I watch you jab, dance and punch at the wind.

    Age just isn't the Southpaw fighter's

        friend.

Bobbin' and weavin'.

    Caught cold a time or two,

    you just keep on going

the distance. Palooka you say, who?

    The years have moved on.

        so much time has passed.

How many more blows

    can you withstand?

        How much longer can

the matches last?

    You're much slower now.

        The fight's in the twelfth round,

way beyond punch drunk,

        Refusing to be knocked down.

        Refusing to stay down.

The fight for now is over.

    The match has reached its end.

    Watching

what could have been

    the world's greatest

        left-handed contender, tirelessly

boxing at the wind

A whole lifetime spent

boxing the wind.

cjj '18

It's so Hard to Say Goodbye to Yesterday

Dese Bones gwine Rise Again...

"Mother"
(Mommy's Poem)

It's been said that

    A-n-g-e-l-s

Are messengers from

    God

Sent from Heaven

    to deliver,

protect, and keep close

    Watch.

Don't you know that

    A-n-g-e-l-s

are really delicate,

    earthly

beings we lovingly

    call

mommy, mom and

M-o-t-h-e-r.

cjj '01

"The Essence of Beauty"

A rain shower of

    Love, Humility and

        Virtue embrace your every

            Step.

Mustard seeds of Faith

    Meekness, and Patience

        were planted by your gentle

            Hands.

You are the essence

    of all that

        is Beautiful, Joyful,

            Peaceful and Kind.

In all Goodness

    and Temperance, you

        prepared me well

        for life's most

Amazing journey,

Living.

You are my mother,

and with the

waking of each new day,

I am made anew

with the Strength and Power

of your Love.

cjj '03

"Remembering Camelot"
(Antoine's Poem I)

Do you remember Camelot?

Arise, big brother. Let us rebuild our

   majestic, magical city.

Let us revisit the innocence of childhood folly.

   I've brought all the things we'll need for our

journey.

Look, I am Lady Guinevere standing by your side.

   Behold, thou art king of all earthly kings,

mighty King Arthur.

   Do you remember Camelot?

Arise, big brother. Take my hand. I can see the

mote

   surrounding the castle.

Can you see the beginnings of our City?

   Let us play as we did when we were once

children.

Let us make folly. Big brother, arise. Let us revisit Camelot.

cjj '97

"A Wish for Tony"
(Antoine's Poem II)

Wishing I could

see your

      smile.

Wishing you well

and an extended

      life.

Wishing you would

      awaken,

my beloved brother

      and

open your eyes.

cjj '98

"Unenduring Torment"

In a single moment of finality, our

    lives are forever changed.

All at once we are forced to live without the

    people we love most in the world.

Life after they are taken away is less.

    Less laughter.

      Less happy.

        Less fulfilling.

No one tells the grieving that the years that

    remain do not get better with time.

We merely learn to accept living our lives with
less.

    When people we love are taken away,

those of us left behind become the walking dead.

    The best part of who we are and were goes

with our dearly departed into the dark, cold

ground.

Each hellacious hour, minute, second and day without our loved ones is an

unenduring torment.

Tell me, how you go on in life

when the best part of who you are, and were has been placed in the dark and cold ground?

cjj'18

You Should Be Mine

Abide with Me...

"Warring Members"

My arms

    long to embrace

        you

My hands

    wish to be held

        by yours

My eyes

    want to behold you

        forever,

today, tomorrow; for always,

        my love.

My lips

    long to kiss

        you

My ears

    wish to hear

you speak

because of you, my

heart and mind

remain in mortal war

today, tomorrow, for always,

my love.

cjj '98

"Dark Gable"

I close my eyes and visualize

    Cocoa skin and bedroom eyes.

There you are in plain sight with

    sleekly loc'd hair and a smile so right,

invading my thoughts and sleepless

       nights,

    invading my thoughts and sleepless

       nights.

Standing tall and perfectly lean,

    the man I envision, the man of my dreams.

The faintest scent of Egyptian musk

    seduces my being with a sweet nocturnal
hush.

There you stand, regally in plain sight;

    invading my thoughts and sleepless

       nights,

invading my thoughts and sleepless

nights.

With a flash of the wind, I quickly open my eyes.

My fantasy ended, Dark Gable vanished,

and he never said goodbye.

cjj '02

"A Blazing Love Affair"

Wrap me up in the

    blanket

        of your love.

Lull me with the

    warmth

        of your smile.

Caress me with the

    sensuality

        of your gaze.

Black man, let us ignite the

Fiery, passionate flame of an

    interminable,

        torrid,

            salacious,

    love affair.

                cjj '97

"Wish list"

Wishing on

    Falling

      stars.

Wishing that

    pots of gold

were really found beneath

    rainbows.

Wishing for

    world peace

      and

    human equality.

Wishing that

    People you love

most in the world

    Mothers, fathers, family and

friends would live

forever.

Wishing for

Complete permanence

in love.

Wishing that

you would

accept the love

I have to give.

Wishing mostly, that I belonged

to you.

cjj '97

Love Don't Love You

I'm Troubled in Mind...

"International Casanova"

Let me be perfectly clear, you really played
yourself.

Do I look like I'm in the mood to deal
with your nonsense today?

That would be a resounding no.

I am not Bank of America, and magical fairies

aren't hiding out in my wallet, creating

money like fairy dust to make your frivolous

dreams come true.

You earned that read and then some.

I mean really, what nerve.

When you promote yourself in excess all over

social media, don't look wounded when

I draw the line at your attempted victimization

of ME.

I will not be supplementing your monetary

shortfall today.

My advice to the International Casanova, you

probably should stay off social media promoting

yourself. It is truly quite revealing.

Italy is very expensive, but sweetheart, when I tell
you

that I can't be your personal golden goose, I

mean that. You have me confused with

Rumpelstiltskin, and I absolutely am not able

to spin straw into gold to furnish your return

from traveling abroad living expenses.

You, sir, have totally earned the full vent of my

attitude, wrath and ire.

Today, you played yourself, and I am one full and

completely fed up black woman.

cjj'18

"Diminished"

I'm definitely checking you out. Just watching,

saying very little, mostly observing the shift
in paradigm of your complicated mindset.

Trying to figure out exactly where it all

went so wrong.

When did I fall from the center of your

universe?

Was it all of a sudden that my value
declined, lessened, decreased; just simply

diminished?

Yes I'm still quietly and silently observing you,

and I have reached a few conclusions of my

own.

Your shift in mindset is not of my lacking.

You see, your waning interest has everything to

do with your less than impressive place in

my world.

You simply are not as significant to me as you once were.

There is definitely a change in paradigm.

Lately, I have discovered the change is mine.

cjj '17

"The End of a Love-Affair"

I've had it…I've really and truly had it.

No more falling head over heels, hopelessly

Devoted to YOU; train wreck out of control, love trips…

I'm done with falling for individuals who refuse to and are incapable of loving ME back. I've had enough of one-sided love affairs.

My knees are all battered and bruised with the whole *please baby, please baby, please, begging routine*. You want to leave.

You want out…Free yourself…GO!

Please return my front door key to the night table before you leave. You probably should call next week, to make arrangements to retrieve the rest of your belongings.

Then again, maybe I won't return them to you, after all.

You were selfish, extremely vain and a completely uninspired lover. You never could fully appreciate Miles Davis and Ralph Ellison, anyway.

Everything considered...I don't think I'll be packing up that box of CD's and books after all. Just return the front door key to the night table on your way OUT!

cjj '98

"Cooled Love"

You don't love me like you used to,

    there's no sparkle in your eyes.

We don't hold hands anymore.

    What happened to the music in my heart

at the mention of your name?

    Our love has cooled.

Our love has changed.

    You don't love me like you used to.

I see it in your eyes. I see it in your smile.

    I feel it on your lips when you kiss me

goodbye.

    Something is different. We're just not the

same.

    Our love has cooled.

    Our love has changed.

There's no melody in my heart at the mention

of your name.

Yes, I guess it's pretty obvious.

Our love has cooled.

Our love has changed.

cjj '02

"Contemplation"

The unyielding cross-roads

    of terminating a tepid

        love-affair

that has simply run its course.

    When the heart tells

        the mind there's

nothing left to fight for

    and you just can't

        make sense

of why anymore.

                cjj '18

"Canceled Carats"

Let us discuss the state of our love.

    Screaming, shouting.

I'm right, you're wrong.

    I know the verse, man, I wrote the song.

Yelling, crying

    You're right, I'm wrong.

A different chorus, but the same

    old song.

Please reconsider the state of our love.

    There's really no need for you

to pack your bags.

    After all, you're being a bit hasty

when you declare you're thinking about

    cancelling the carats.

                cjj '98

"State of Indifference"

Just keeping it honest and real.

    You want me all up in

my feelings, somehow that

    makes it about you.

What I now am is indifferent.

    That's all one hundred

        about me.

Indifference is really a dangerous

    place for emotion

        to rest.

Indifference is the disinterested

    state where people

        place you

right before they move on

    from you

and out of

your life.

cjj '18

Can We Talk?

He Never Said A Mumbling Word...

"Paramount Workmanship"

You can't dull my shine

    no matter how hard

you try.

    It was given to me from

my Creator, the maker

    and giver of life.

I was made in his image,

    bearing his likeness and

similitude. That's the reason

    why you hate me and

don't understand my unapologetically

    black, and majestic attitude.

Be mindful how you treat me.

    Consider your evil ways.

I am the paramount workmanship

    of my everlasting Father,

the ancient of days.

So while you hating on me,

the Good Book says you should

be loving me.

Careful, I'm the apple of my

maker's eye.

Made to shine brighter than the stars

that light up the never-ending

sky.

Stop blaming, shaming, and

renaming me.

I was fashioned in God's image.

That's why you can't dull my shine.

I'm fueled by the power of the stone

of Israel since before clocks could

keep imperfect time.

You can't contain the light or block

out my shine, it was first formed

by my Creator long before clocks could keep

imperfect time.

cjj '18

"Inner Galactic Love Scene"

Black man, you are the eighth, ninth and tenth

    wonder of the

        world.

With eyes so bright and a smile

    that transcends this immediate

        hemisphere.

You are cosmically divine.

    Can we share an inner galactic
        love scene?

Somewhere…

    Anywhere…

        beneath the sun,

moon

  and

    heavenly stars…

cjj '99

"The Proposition"

You passed by me one day

and my knees felt weak.

I mean, I watched you walk

two blocks before it occurred to me

that I just gazed upon the finest

specimen of black masculinity

in its purest form. What I'm trying

to tell you is: man, you are fine…and if

you're free tonight, maybe we could converse

with one another over dinner.

If time won't permit that, let's exchange ideas

on religion and politics over a drink.

And maybe if you're not too busy, say over the

next lifetime or so, we could fall

madly, passionately, and completely in love.

cjj '97

"Galaxy Mack"

I am femininity defined,

    Venus.

Second planet from the

    Sun.

You are Mars, a celestially

    masculine body

with earth and other relative

    matter

standing between us.

Tell me, how can our two separate

    planets occupy the same shared

      Space?

Suga, I know your troposphere is

beneath my mesosphere.

    I've heard all that before.

I know all the different variables

surrounding, revolving and separating our

Stratosphere.

That aside, how do we get our two separate

planets to occupy the same shared

Space?

I know that you're the fourth planet from the

Sun,

But can't you see that I'm trying to make

You a distinguished part of my own personal

Assembly?

Man, I want you solely, wholly,

completely, encompassing my

Universe.

cjj '97

"One Indian Summer Night"

We sat on a bench one

Indian summer

night,

and spoke of life, love, our hopes and dreams.

All in time was still.

Smooth, hushed, breezes.

Autumn leaves settled on the ground.

You held my hand,

my soul felt light.

All in time was still.

A soft-spoken, man with gentle eyes,

an understanding heart.

For just one moment

all was perfect in my

world.

You gave me Camelot.

.

cjj '97

'Til You Do Me Right

How Long...

"25 Years of Crisis-Filled Lives"

Are you really going to stand there

and just pour out all

the refuse of your life

on the floor of my living room?

I don't have it in me today.

Didn't bring no vacuum,

didn't bring no broom.

Just poured out all your garbage
right on the floor of my living room.

I can't be your psychoanalyst.

Dr. Phil moved to a different network

and my name ain't Iyanla.

Chile, I can't fix your life.

I don't have it in me. No, not today.

Can't you see the pail is full? It's
overflowing

on the floor of my living room,

my living room.

25 years of crisis-filled lives is too great

a burden for

any one soul to bear

25 years of cleaning up

your garbage.

God knows, I got more than my share.

You never even offered me a garbage

bag or can.

It's time for me to end this,

make some new demands.

Ours has been a one-sided
relationship.

I got nothing more to give.

Sometimes family can be

the greatest drain of all.

One continuous, endless sieve.

I accept y'all think I'm the fix it all,

make it feel good,

clean-up woman.

But there's no "S" upon my chest.

I'm closing my door, showing

you the way out

25 years of cleaning up

crisis-filled lives

I know I've earned my rest.

cjj '18

"Full Circle"
(Jazz's Poem: The Story of Us)

I was there for all the monumental parts of your

life.

Birthdays, prom, Chris Brown

concerts,

high school graduation and going off

to college trunk parties.

Do you remember me?

I was front row then when all that mattered

was made available for you.

Now that you have grown

up and reached a

certain place in our life, I have been dismissed.

No fanfare or communication.

No heartfelt goodbyes.

Only empty, unfulfilled

promises with zero commitment and

even less effort.

I have now been granted far back

row access to your life,

and frankly speaking, that

just isn't good enough. I won't accept your

after-thought undertaking.

In time you will know what I'm
feeling.

"If youth but knew what age could tell."

The child that you're bringing into

the world will invariably treat

you the same way.

Karma indeed the "living well."

You'll understand my perspective then.

When you become the far back row
observer in your child's adult life,

---

all of this; us, you and I, will become full circle.

You will remember me then.

cjj '17

"Exhausted Black Barista"

I am a simmering tea kettle boiling over.

So sick of everyone's rotten,

spoiled tea.

Doesn't matter the brand, it's all

just spilling over, and I am

way too full.

Bigelow is bitter, Lipton too cheap.

Tired of all this rancid caffeine

starting to affect my sleep.

If you can't stand the heat, exit the

kitchen.

Well, I have left the

kitchen and removed

the oven mittens.

I can't tolerate the drama you like

Serving while you're

Spilling all of your tea.

Just take it all with you when

you leave.

Quit bothering me.

Don't want it served up hot,

can't stand it warm or cold.

No, thank you. Please

keep your Teavana it too, is

way too old.

Honey, young and restless is

way out of date.

Your drama is tired.

It's getting late.

I don't care how you pour it,

I'm just too full.

Sick of your drama, tired of the bull.

The kitchen is closed, the

mugs have been put away.

Turning off the lights now,

unbelievably shaking my head.

The hour is late it's time

for me to go to bed.

Can't you see it's getting late?

Tomorrow's another day,

Chile, the Black Barista

really can't do the putrid

screen-play of your messy life.

Please just keep it moving I say.

cjj '18

Unchain My Heart

My Way is Cloudy...

"Precipice of Heartbreak"

Tumbling down an emotional cliff

without a safety net or

parachute.

Completely gone.

I am

so lost

in you.

cjj '18

"Lamenting Love"

I would have done anything and everything for

     you;

lassoed the moon, boarded the fastest rocket

     to bring you the farthest star.

Lately, I've been thinking about how undignified

     our love has become.

It's hard to remember sexy phone calls in the

     middle of the night.

I can't recall holding hands or walks through the

     park.

Lately, I've been thinking about your

     absence from me, what it all means...I guess

I am lamenting our love.

     Remembering, remembering the way we

used to be.

cjj '97

"Silent Deliberation"

Remember when you used to stare at me for no

apparent reason?

Seconds, minutes, hours your eyes were locked on

Mine,

but that was long ago.

Do you remember when you placed me
right in the center of your universe?

The morning greeting and smile that

found me at sunrise packed up and moved to a

different continent.

No forwarding number or mailing address

could be found.

I never saw the moving van arrive.

You left swiftly, in silent deliberation.

I never saw it coming.

You left quietly, I was broken,

completely destroyed and you

never said a word.

cjj '99

"469 Days Ago"

When was the last time

    you kissed me deeply,

held my hand,

    loved me completely?

When was the last time

    you held me tightly,

whispered sweet nothings,

    said that you loved me?

When was the last time

    you caressed my hair

or embraced me gently?

    469 days ago,

You held me close. You loved me then…

    Passionately, Passionately.

cjj '02

"Dream a Dream of Me"

I want to be the first thought on your mind

     and every thought in between.

I want to be the reason you wake up, the reason

     that you breathe.

I want to be the rainbow in your life after a

     summer rain. I'd like to be one with you in
joy. Let me comfort all your pain.

     I want to be the sunshine, the stars within

your sky. The one who makes you laugh,

     that holds you when you cry.

I want to be the last thought on your mind before

     you go to sleep,

the woman you adore who visits all your dreams.

cjj '97

"The Things I Don't Remember"

Since your departure, all thoughts of you
have faded from my memory.

I don't remember your squared,
dimpled chin, nor

do I recall your flawless state of dress.
I don't remember the way your soft, curly hair felt

resting on my fingertips. I don't remember
gentle, silky kisses on my right shoulder

as you greeted me with good morning.
I don't remember the lingering smell of your

bath soap or aftershave.
I don't remember the eight tiny crinkles that

formed in the corners of your eyes when you
smiled, nor do I recall the four hairs of your

mustache which refused to keep
perfect order.

I don't remember the way you whispered

"goodnight Sweetheart" in my ear before you drifted off to sleep.

Since your departure…No, I can't say that I remember anything about you at all.

cjj '97

"Black Clouds"

Have you ever noticed,

    when staring

        out of a moving car window,

the muted pain of

    a melancholy,

        lonely, lovesick, heart

fades into the air

    of night

        like one big, black, fluffy,

puff of smoke?

cjj '99

"Life's Luster Lost"

Nothing is the same.

Sunny days,

ice cream sundaes,

old movie classics,

that we used to watch on tv.

Nothing is the same.

Neighborhood gossip,

familiar places,

friendly faces,

dance music bumping and loud

at the old stomping ground.

Nothing is the same,

absolutely, nothing.

My existence in life is so much more dismal and

lonely with your not being here.

cjj '98

"Twenty-Year Flashback"

Ours was the love affair that wasn't.

A twenty-year memory of longing for
the one that got away.

Funny, as the days and years go by,
I'm reminded of what could have been.

Lost in yesterday, recalling the possibility
of *what if we had worked*? Have the years been

kind to you, or have you become someone
I can no longer recognize? Time is a bittersweet

cruelty. It has a way of moving on, but the
heart is still held captive by stilled thoughts and

unrelenting memories of you. Twenty years
too late on a sunny afternoon, flashbacks of us hit

me and I am completely overtaken by past
memories of our yesterday. A willing prisoner of

lost days gone by. The unfulfilled possibility
of what could have been you and me.

cjj '18

You Bring Me Joy

Oh Happy Day...

"Rainbow of my Soul"

You are the rainbow,

     the luster,

the jewel

     within my sky.

The magic,

     the splendor,

the love of my life.

     You are the reason my

Soul glides

     upon air

Yours is the life, I long to share,

     to love,

to hold,

     to cherish

and console.

An arc of brilliant color,

you're the rainbow

of my soul.

cjj '97

"Twinkle, Twinkle"

Shimmery, Gleaming

    Sparkly

and

    Bright

Dazzling, Magnificent;

    More radiant than

Sunlight.

    Glimmery, Splendid,

Blazing

    what Shine

Twinkling little moon beams;

    My Sweetheart's

Beautiful

    Brown

eyes.

              cjj '98

"The Romance Thing"

It's kind of smooth the way

you stand up from the table

to pull out my chair

    when I feel the need

      to excuse myself.

I dig the way you lay a napkin

across my lap as to protect my

clothing from food

    particles.

It's kind of fly when you open

up doors, pick up fallen hankies

    from the floor, and

    straight up do that

    gentleman thing that you do.

So your vibin' off my femininity.

Yeah, I'm vibin' off your masculinity,

And just maybe, perhaps with all

the things that we're vibin' on,

we'll get this

Romance thing Right.

cjj '97

"Love-Filled Greetings"

Dancing on air.

Flashes of you

come to mind.

Sending out love-filled greetings

and heart-shaped bouquets

because I love and

want to be near you

Because…Because…Because…

cjj '98

"Chronic Sleeplessness"

Lying in my bed at night

    Dreamy thoughts of you

Morning moves to 3:00 a.m.

    Tick tock, tick tock

The constant clicking of the clock

What are you doing?

    Sleeping I suppose

Lying quietly in your bed

    while perfectly smoothed sheets hug

your lean, brown, body.

My, how I wish I were the

    perfectly fluffed pillow

that envelops your sleekly loc'd hair.

Tick tock, tick tock

The constant clicking of the clock.

cjj '99

"The Seasons of My Love"

Everything about you is marked by a notable amount

of heat.

You are Summer love.

With lips sweeter than the ripest honey-dew melon.

I kiss you and explode.

Hot, hot, very hot. You're so hot.

You make me hot.

Everything about you is marked by a tremendous

amount of change.

You are my Autumn love.

Your kiss has changed, no longer to be identified.

Your moods shift quicker than Autumn leaves

Modify their colors and fall

to the ground.

Changing, changing, our love is always changing.

You, coming and going leaving me hanging.

Maybe it's time I do some rearranging.

My, how quickly our love has cooled.

Your kiss is not the same.

Lately, everything about you is marked by a

deficiency of warmth.

You are my Winter love.

You're cold, and this has nothing to do with

inclement weather or sub-zero temperatures.

Cold, cold, oh so cold.

After loving you, I almost froze.

Hot and cold, sometimes lukewarm with the

faintest

memory of a gentle Spring.

These are the seasons of my love.

cjj '97

"The Kiss"

It began with a mutual

magnetic attraction.

Two impeccable silhouettes

standing in the distance.

The intense gaze of the eyes.

An uncontested closeness of shared space,

And within one anticipated moment,

it happened.

A sweet, impassioned kiss.

cjj '97

"Sweet Mocha Chocolate"

I want my man cerebral

on the straight up hip tip.

    Hypnotically charismatic

with an acid jazz funk.

    Say brother, leave the ego tripping to me,

I'd like to think I do it much better.

    I want him no nonsense,

in yo' face, with a this is

    how I am, black woman flavor.

He's got to be smooth, with

    an earthy sensibility.

Feeling what I'm feeling

    as I'm feeling him.

Essentially, I want my man as

    soothing to my soul as

sweet mocha chocolate

sliding down your throat

on a cool Autumn day.

cjj '97

"Reflections of You"

Living in the

    moment.

Catching a winter

    breeze.

Thinking about my

Baby puts my mind at

    ease.

Riding on a

    Wave.

Drifting on a

    love-high.

Remembering the warmth

of your kiss.

Writing poems about

my sweetheart,

the love of my

life.

cjj '98

"Recalling Heaven"

Take me to a

    place

that's warm, fuzzy and

    bright.

Where love abounds and

    my heart is held

captive

    by the flame of your

fervently, brazen, kiss.

cjj '98

"The Music of My Soul"

Sam Cooke

    crooned

"You Send Me."

    Simply put,

        you spin me

wh-ew-ww-ww,

    Brotha's off da

        chain.

You sent Stokley

    swangin'

        crucial stylo bangin'

Earth Wind & Fire

    said it best, "Gotta

        Get You into my Life."

cjj '01

"Your Place"

The vivid scent of citrus orchards fully fills

my space.

Thinking of you. Meditating on love.

Thoughts of you in your place.

Tranquil sounds of oriental music

remain in my head.

Green, soft, satin, pillows resting on your bed.

Sweet, romantic, sonnets surround me in

my space.

Thinking of you.

A beautiful black artist creating

visions of you in your place.

Glowing rays of sunshine dance across the sky.

Thoughts of us embracing

quickly come to mind.

The vibrant smell of orange groves wholly

fills my space.

    Thinking of you still.

Meet me at your place.

cjj '97

What's Love Got to do With It

Ain't Gonna Let Nobody Turn Me Roun'...

"Woman"

I am more than the sum

    of my body parts.

        I am divine.

Transcending all

    space and time.

        My beginnings are

ever of old,

        eclipsing the

            African Nile.

I acquired knowledge

    of life's intricate path at

        King Solomon's feet.

I am divine.

    Transcending all

        space and time.

From the hypnotic

and mesmerizing sway of

    my hips, men throughout

the ages were brought

    to their knees.

      All nations came from

the bowels of my Mother Eve.

    She was taken right from my

      Father Adam's side.

They are supreme, giving

    life and form to every living

      God-breathing thing.

You marvel at my ancestry

    while coveting my majesty;

      Hating what you can't

understand.

    God-made, black

    "don't crack."

Hair that defies gravity

and melanin that has never

regarded science.

Admittedly, quite hard to

comprehend.

I am more than the sum

of my body parts.

I am divine.

Transcending all

space and time.

My father first called me

woman.

cjj '18

"Eluding Slumber"

Days melt into darkness.

    I simply am unable to speak.

Disappointment and despair have

    hijacked any illusion of

rest my soul desperately

    seeks to find.

Slumber so far away now,

    an impending impossibility.

Morning looms upon the horizon.

    Nighttime a faded memory.

I am still held hostage

    from a lack of sleep.

Suddenly, my tongue is

    loosed all at once.

Unspoken words spring forth

from the belly of my soul.

Unshed tears begin to fall

and the words poured out.

cjj'18

"Summer Farewell"

Burnt orange Autumn leaves

    fall slowly to the ground,

        leaving behind quiet

Summer memories of ruby-throated

    hummingbirds and the

        faintest scent of

jasmine vines.

                cjj '18

"Broken"

Shattered dreams of unfulfilled

hope,

grabbing desperately at anything,

something.

Spiraling down the unassailable

Mountain of defeat,

collecting fragments of

deferred dreams.

Beaten, bruised,

down on my knees.

Picking up the pieces

of a fragile, broken, life.

cjj '98

"Unfulfilled"

Wanting.

    Spending an entire lifetime

        wanting.

When will it finally be our turn to

    have something,

        anything?

Are deferred dreams ever realized?

    Wanting, ever wanting

        days and nights

Wanting.

    King Solomon called it outright,

        that which is wanting

        cannot be numbered.

Days and nights

    still

        wanting.

           cjj'18

"Waiting"

Waiting is so passé. It's occurred to me that I've

    spent the majority of my life waiting.

Waiting on buses, trains and planes. Waiting on

    untelevised revolution.

Waiting on payday. Waiting to have my dreams,

    and ambitions fulfilled.

Waiting on reciprocated adoration and respect

    from unworthy lovers.

Lately, I find myself waiting on your infrequent

    phone calls.

Waiting for you to appear on my doorstep

    on-time, which you never seem to do.

Waiting to hear the pathetically, lame excuses, as

    to why you continually disrespect my time.

Recently, I've had a rather ablutionary revelation.

Simply put, your time is up.

Black Man, I will no longer wait for You.

cjj '97

"Princess of the Magnificent Mile"

I saw her walking in beauty and perfect light,

    grace and elegance

        burned in her eyes.

She walked with confidence, a regal air,

    her head held high,

        kissing rich, blue, skies.

I tell you I've seen her somewhere

    before.

Poetry in motion and so much more.

    She walked in beauty with

        her head held high.

A perfectly- fashioned,

    beautiful, black, French tulip

        walking as if she owned

the Magnificent Mile.

        cjj'98

"Hump day Blues"

This is what's real, and what's real is this:

    the discovery of your living in

Midweek Wednesday,

    Feeling as if it were

blue Monday,

    and the surreal notion

of wishing it

    were Friday

shrouds every pore of your being

    and every pattern of your

natural thought process.

Can I get a witness…a witness…one single
witness…

    a witness…a witness?

One lone witness.

cjj '97

"The Sum Total of Three"

One plus one makes two.

    I'm always the added extra number;

my sum total equals three.

    Three is always a crowd.

The added extra number is always

    the odd one left out;

the third wheel with no designated

    space or place.

Always, always, left over

    and usually left

Alone.

cjj '98

"A Visit to the Library"

This time around, love has left me with a bitter

taste in my mouth.

Robbed. Robbed of all feeling, void of all emotion.

No peace or rest do I find.

You're an unconscionable thief taking what you

want, only to sell it to the nearest pawnshop
for the lowest price.

The next time around, I will be leery of tall,
good-looking black men bearing promises of

unyielding love.

The next time I decide to venture off to the library,

I will be certain to only bring home the
books.

cjj '97

"Script Flipping"

You flipped the script. Don't you understand

    in my draft of the screenplay

you were Sir Lancelot?

    Gallant, chivalrous, a courtly pursuer of all

that is romantic and grand about love.

    You flipped the script. You are no Lancelot.

Behold, a lowly toad.

    All this time I've been gently kissing you

Hoping for a Prince, a knight, a Sir Lancelot.

    I can't believe that you're really a toad.

cjj '97

"Deliverance"

In the weary, still, quiet of life,

    fearful eyes and feet

hide behind closed doors.

    Hoping,

        praying,

            waiting,

    on deliverance

from a cruel,

    raging,

        savage,

            beast.

cjj '02

The Makings of You

Going to Set Down and Rest a While...

"Upended Universe"
(Micheal's Poem II)

I am made better with your presence in my world.

    Everything shifted in my universe at

your earth-tilting intrusion.

    The sound of your voice enables me to soar.

I can move mountains because you

    tell me that I can.

I am made smaller, taller, less and more

    all at the same time.

I am smarter, bolder, more beautiful and enough

    with your seismic presence in my world.

I am made better.

cjj '18

"Thought Defined"
(Micheal's Poem I)

You are my every logical and illogical

    mental process.

All

    rationalization,

contemplation,

    argumentation and observation.

Every conclusion,

    supposition,

cogitation

    and all understanding.

You are the greatest love

    my life has ever known.

Micheal, you're simply my every thought.

cjj '99

"Lipstick & Crowns"
(Jennifer's Declaration III)

You are light.

A 1500 mega-watt, blinding bright light.

You're a completely flawless, Black radiant

diamond. The rarest kind.

There just isn't another like

you in the world. Keep shining brightly,
darling and never remove your crown.

Always know your value isn't placed in

the hands of others. Continue to carve out your

own unique space in God's amazing world.

When the sometimes turbulent, rains of life begin

falling in yours,

reach for your crown, dearest.

Never lay it down.

Place it upon your perfectly coiffed big, curly,

---

woolly hair and dance your

way right through the storm, just as David danced before the Lord.

You keep dancing, loved one. Never forget you're the daughter of "the king."

Remember these words from your mom, "Life is always made better with a little

lipstick and a smile."
If you ever can't remember or recall who

you are I'm here to help you remember.
Moms have bragging rights. We get to

pretend we had something to do with the
Magnificently illuminating creatures our

adult children become.
Your soul has always been knit with mine.

It will remain that way long after I'm gone.
Keep on dancing, Jennifer and never remove

your crown.

One lifetime in your regal presence is simply

not enough.

I love you always, my beautiful,

precious girl.

cjj '18

"A Child's Poem"
(Isaiah, Joy, Faith & Bella's Poem)

Come ride with me

    on silver-colored ponies

and gossamer wings.

    Let us fly over candy-coated

magical rainbows

    to a place called happily ever after.

Greet me with hugs and kisses

    as we dance by moonlight

in the land of never, never.

    Today, tomorrow, forever and ever.

cjj '97

"Fuchsia Colored Pom-Pons"
(Lauren's Declaration IV)

You were my heart's first love.

A beautifully perfect, chocolate

bundle of joy.

I look at you now all grown up

and it's hard to let go of your

baggy-diapered yesterday.

I can't run your life, but it doesn't stop me

from trying. I am unwillingly letting go.

I accept that you will make your own mistakes.

I certainly did. Promise me you'll always

remember the wise words of your granny, "If you

ask for nothing, you'll get nothing."

Raise your standards, young woman.

You're worth so much more than you

accept.

You were fearfully and wonderfully made. Love is

possible. Love yourself.

Make your demands and never settle for less than

you deserve. Lasso your happiness and

don't entrust it to others.

You're fabulous for such a short time, dear.

Snatch your happy with manicured hands and

always know I'm here for you; the

obnoxiously, loud, overbearing cheerleader

with the fuchsia-colored pom-pons,

lovingly, pushing you across life's

tumultuous finishing line.

cjj'18

"Leopard Print Fashionista"
(India's Declaration V)

How can I reach you? Tell me, how I can make you remember YOU? I would do anything humanly possible to break through that chemically induced haze you've been lost in for years. There is no one more talented, funny or charming than you. I can't understand why you traded in your fabulous for bargain basement skid row. You were the little fashionista sporting leopard print jackets and Baby Phat waist coats. I remember it well.

Flashback yesterday, there once was a very beautiful girl who used to sing off-key to Tevin Campbell songs and create the most amazing art. What happened to that girl?

Flash-forward, now, present time. Maturity knows the years are not kind, they just keep moving along. They don't care about what's been left undone either. Time has a way of going on without you being present.

The saddest part of life for me is watching you aspire to nothing. This is the greatest degradation and devastation of your life, watching unfulfilled potential. I'm here waiting, hoping, praying, for your breakthrough. You can't mask hurt and pain with alcohol and drugs no matter how hard you try.

One day, time eventually catches up to us all. It is quite cruel. The memories aren't as vivid anymore. How do I reach you? Why can't you remember you? I, remember, and it hurts watching you, throw YOU, away. I could tell you all day every day how wonderful you are, but you stopped believing in you a long time ago. Today, right now, I thought I would help you remember.

Should you ever become present enough to start living in this moment and need help with your recall, I will gladly help you remember. I'm here. I have always been right here. I remember *"your fabulous."* I remember all the stuff that you no longer call to mind. You really were the little leopard print fashionista with the *"on fleek"* hairstyle and the dazzling cover girl smile. I remember, India. I remember YOU.

cjj '18

"Golden"

Each and every Saturday, like

    clock work,

        I'm visited by the

           Sun.

Bouncing golden rays of

    sunlight

        glide into my space.

A little boy with curly,

    sandy-colored hair

        and copper skin

gobbles up peppermint candy

    while resting his head

        upon my lap.

He sleeps the afternoon away, and

    patiently, ever so patiently,

I wait for next Saturday to

come.

cjj '98

"A Landscape of Brilliant Color"
(Greg's Poem)

Yesterday we built rainbows and placed

them in the sky,

a landscape of brilliant

color,

together, you and I.

In 60 days, we tenderly fashioned each

delightful bow.

Designed a vibrant blueprint

for happy lovers left below

hues of generosity and kindness

beamed with every ray of light,

and the bows were a little

sadder as they kissed the Sun

goodbye.

cjj '01

Untelevised Revolution

Buked and Scorned...

"Black Folks Tired of Singing We Shall Overcome"

White privilege gives

    you cover.

Your blues ain't

    nothin' like

mine.

    Police don't kill

White people;

    mostly killing

mine.

No justice, No peace.

    Police brutality.

400 years of black lives

    in peril

spawn Black hostility.

    100 years of singing

God bless America,

 let freedom ring;

      while the

world stands by in

      silence,

watching Black suffering.

      You cannot know

The rage I carry, that's

      buried deep inside.

Protesting since King.

      Living separate and

unequal, bloody,

      Black Lives.

               cjj '18

"Black History"

A little black book found in your drawer,

    lying on the table, placed upon a shelf,

open it up and discover yourself.

    Learn about your history, a story new and

old, the story of enslaved Black people

    bought and sold.

HIDDEN in prisons with chains on your feet,

    dazed and confused standing in the streets.

A little black book will tell you who you are,

    scattered here and there under every

heavenly star.

    Priests, prophets, kings and queens; our

heritage is rich with all of these things.

    This little black book translated in every

language, nation and tongue tells the story of God,

    his people and a city, Jerusalem.

A little black book found in your drawer,

lying on the table placed upon a shelf;

open it up and SAVE yourself.

cjj '99

"The Black Fruit Gatherers"

Strange fruit no longer hangs from trees,

it lies in any city street,

outlined with markings of yellow and

orange fluorescent tape.

Age is not a consideration either.

Seemingly, the more tender

The fruit, the better.

The fruit is gathered regardless

of the weather.

The fruit is gathered regardless

of the weather.

Rodney King was at least beaten

within inches of his life.

That wasn't the case for 12-year old

baby boy, Tamir Rice.

We by now all know the familiar

drill, we've seen it all before. Armed,

"trigger-happy" officers donning stiff, blue

uniforms firmly standing their ground.

The homicide scene is always the same.

Another black life gone, a different

Headline name.

Block by block, city by city, unarmed

Black lives abruptly snuffed out.

Makes me want to holler,

Makes me want to shout.

My God, My God, another black life

quickly snuffed out.

Warm and very red blood splatters to the

grey, hard, cold, concrete.

Is that the pungent odor of

magnesium that swiftly fills the air?

Another black life gone, lying in the street.

Not to worry, the fraternal Blue Brotherhood

remains unbothered they haven't a regret,

not one single care. No protection for Black

Lives. They just simply never mattered.

Another black life gone, lying in the street.

The fruit is gathered regardless

of the weather.

The fruit is gathered regardless

of the weather.

Police sirens sound, announcing the

arrival of the strange fruit gatherers.

They show up poised with weapons

drawn,

hastily prepared to gather more Black fruit.

hurriedly prepared to gather more Black fruit.

cjj '18

"Why We Can't Salute Oppression"

White privilege allows your guilt-free conscience

      to not consider that you're

indeed my oppressor.

      For this reason, you hide behind

patriotism and insist that I must do so too.

      I cannot pledge allegiance to a country

or flag that never pledged allegiance to me.

      This is why you refuse to honor

or understand my protest bowed, not standing;

      down on bended knee.

2017 the oppressor is still very much

      content with my oppression,

because black lives only matter

      when white lives can monetarily benefit

from the pain, pillage, and suffering of

400 years of black inequality.

cjj '17

"Revolution: '97 Style"

Nikki, it's 1997 and I'm still waiting for revolution.

Waiting…waiting…waiting…yes, waiting 27
long years for untelevised revolution.

Nigga can you kill? Can a nigga kill?

Will you defend yourselves by any means

necessary?

Once the revolution takes place, black people tell

me, will you defend yourselves?

Martin and Malcolm are long gone and brotha's

Are still getting beat over their heads with
sticks.

Gone are the days of the crisp, white sheet,
whitey hides behind a shiny, silver badge and a

cop's uniform.

Just ask Rodney, now that brotha never got the

chance to defend himself.

I'm all for Revolution, televised or not. Let's set it

off '97 style.

Revolution…Revolution…Revolution…Yeah,

Bring on the Revolution.

I'm with Gil, it doesn't have to be televised.

I've just grown tired of waiting.

Nikki, aren't you tired of waiting?

Still waiting…waiting…waiting

27 long years for

untelevised Revolution.

cjj '97

"Definitely Team Kaep"

It was never about patriotism

    or disrespecting a flag.

It wasn't about the raised fists

    held high up in the air

or our big, round circular hair.

    It has always been about

straight equality.

    Stop murdering black folks.

Stop killing me.

    No justice, No Peace.

Whether marching, sitting in, or

    down on bended knee.

Stop murdering black folks.

    Stop killing me.

I will not shut up and play football

    with black blood

staining the streets.

I will not stand in silence

while white folks killing me.

cjj'18

"Color Me Black"

Color me black

    cause that's what I be.

Whitey can never,

    ever be me.

Don't strut like me.

    or flow like me.

Like Ellison said, whitey

    don't even see me.

I am invisible 'cept' for when whitey

    robbin', beatin', or jailin' me.

Color me black

    cause that's what I be.

Dark as pitch, precious like

    an onyx stone.

Don't need whitey to understand me,

    just leave me alone.

Let me be. Cause when we interact,

you, plottin', schemin', and

exploitin' my ethnicity.

Color me black

cause that's what I be.

Sun-kissed black skin

like Solomon.

You know, the real, black, dope

King of Israel.

That's who my peoples be.

but black folks don't read

their history.

cjj '99

"The Black Condition"

Dred Scott

    Ku Klux Klan

Marchin' in the street

    Jim Crow

We shall overcome

    P-O-L-I-C-E B-R-U-T-A-L-I-T-Y

Lost history

    Bigotry

Black folks go to jail

    Poverty

Millennium year 2001

    BLACK FOLKS IN C-A-P-T-I-V-I-T-Y

cjj '01

"272 Years of Unsung Independence"

There's something else going on. Us Black folks

  have known it for way too long.

See, our unsung pursuit of happiness is under

  mortal threat.

Living while Black will get the police called on

  you quicker than any named committed
crime ever could.

  Let me make the case.

Can't grab coffee at Starbucks no more while

  Black.

Nope, taking walks in your neighborhood while

  Black

will result in police sirens and shake downs, that's

  just plain ole simple fact.

Barbecuin' in the park with yo family while Black,

  we absolutely don't dare do that.

Let me play it back just to be certain you're really

feelin', me.

Drivin', walkin', sleepin', shoppin', and sittin',

While Black

will result in unwarranted contact with

trigger-happy police.

Yet, I'm expected not to react?

Yet, I'm expected not to react?

When white police interact with Black folks, that

very well might be our last interaction

in life. Ya dig? Y' all feelin' me?

White folks know this too. Still, regardless of
where we live Black reality.

Was this the intent of the founding fathers
272 years ago?

Let's talk about inalienable rights of
happiness, life and liberty again...

Who declared rights and independence for
Black folks?

Cause where I'm standing, in the Black skin

I'm in, White folks have placed my happiness

Under Mortal threat.

Living while Black has become White folks'

unnecessary casualty, and that's

as real as real can get.

cjj '18

Still the BaddDDDest

People Around

Lift Every Voice and Sing...

"Ode to Sonia"

Sonia, you are the baddDDDest, the absolute

    dopest

chick since before and after the

      rebirth of Harlem.

    I'm talking as phaatt as any dame can be.

Rolling up on the set bold as any dude,

    flaunting your ethnicity with much attitude.

Now Nikki is flyy and Gwen is all that, but

    personally, girl, you way baddDDDer and

that's just an undisputed fact.

    Your thots, your words

are as cold as can be;

    causing emotions to stir

      celebrating black ethnicity.

Setting free my soul, wh-ee-ww-eee, my soul is

    free,

free in my blackness, free in me.

Chile, I'm free. Free to roam, free to chill,

to unapologetically be black

and that's straight up for real.

Yep, Sonia got it going on this is no lie

writing 'bout' black thots. Now tell me,

ain't that flyy?

Girl, you're dope. Feeling our pain. I said it before,

You're one baddDDD dame.

Yeah, Sonia you real baddDDD,

and you be getting baddDDDer in my world

every day.

cjj '97

"Salutation"
(For Black Men Everywhere)

I've just got to proclaim, exclaim and call you by

name:

Maleek, Dion, Amir and Tyrone,

Darrell, Hakeem, Zarif, and Ramone.

This is for all the def brothers who

got it goin' on

and on and on.

The brothers are fine. The brothers are fly.

Thinking about super fine

Black men makes me high.

Sporting their fros, locs, waves and fades.

Physiques like Shaka Zulu.

Coming in every shade.

Reddish brown, bluish black,

copper and yellow,

packin' much back.

Let the sisters shout. Let us declare

the beauty of brothers everywhere.

Hoopin' on the court

Pushing shopping carts

wearing Armani suits

breakin' many hearts.

Hanging at the club or hanging on the street

Kicking much game, speaking your

rhythmic speech.

Yeah, sisters be watchin'

And blondie be jockin',

sizing you up, scheming and plotting.

But this ain't about blondie

or exposing her plan,

this is a salutation of love and respect

revering the Black man.

Let the sisters proclaim, exclaim,

stating all that we feel.

Loving our brothers

Infinitely.

Keepin' it real.

cjj '97

Black Expression
Volume II

Always Look Towards Zion

I Shall Not Be Moved...

Lyris D. Wallace

Dedication

I would like to dedicate this book to my son, Jonah, I hope when the world gets cold and dark, that he picks up this book and remembers he's loved and finds comfort and warmth in his mother's words.

Acknowledgements

To my son, Jonah Wallace-Young, thank you for giving me purpose and direction. You are always my compass that leads me back home. Love you to the ends of the earth and back.

Dad, Sylvester S. Wallace, thank you for buying my favorite fairytale book and "encouraging" me to read with everyone in the family over and over and over again.

Mommy, Edna M. Wallace, thank you for buying the "Nancy Drew and Hardy Boys Mysteries" book series as well as "Are you There God, It's Me Margaret" book series.

I thank my brother, Antoine M. Wallace, for always believing and encouraging me, when I didn't believe in myself.

My sisters:

Felicia Wallace, thanks for inspiring what I feel are some of my best poems. Keep fighting, keep striving for improvement, and keep giving me inspiration.

Chyrel J. Jackson, thanks for spear-heading this project, and believing in the both of us. Thank you for all your support, love, and advice through the years. I think you know I couldn't get along without you.

Mr. Thomas Young, my father-in-law, thank you for filling in the gap all these years. Jonah and I love and appreciate you so very much.

Thank you to the rest of my friends, especially the Brantley's who gave my son and I a safe place, when we had no place. Love you guys so much. Yours is a friendship I will always treasure.

08/05/99
12:31pm

"The Other Half of Myself"

I'm not as tall as you,
      as smart as you,
      as radiant as you,
I'm not as kind as you,
      as soft as you,
      as giving as you.
I don't move like you,
      walk like you,
      laugh like you.
I don't even look like you,
      talk like you,
      have hair like you
      or smell like you,
But, I am You
      And You are Me,
      And We are One.
For We are two Halves
      Of one Whole
And you are what I hope to be.

Express Yo' self

Old Zion's Children Marching Along...

11/03/00
10:10pm

"Take the Mountains Slowly: For Jonah"

How can my pen write what is so deeply felt in
my heart?
You are a walking reality of my sweetest dream.
A frustration of hope,
A worry of peace,
A sigh of joy and laughter.
My tomorrows are in the brightness of your smile.
My todays are in the prayers of your tomorrow's.
I am eager to teach you the lessons for your life's
journey.
My heart beats with anticipation of your travels.
Hopefully, my lessons will be your map,
and my heart will be your compass.
May love and peace be your companions,
hope and desire your strength,
and joy and laughter your peace.
Take the mountains slowly.
Examine all the paths carefully before you,
and always look toward Zion.
Love Always, Momma

01/01/99
11:57pm

"Words I Dare Not Speak"

My reality is bleak,
My moments are long.
Each tick of the clock is a betrayal.
I look for comfort and there is only a second hand
moving slowly to the bong of another hour.
The voices are long, slurred illusions;
Whispering words, each syllable cutting deeper.
This reality is a nightmare I cannot wake from,
A beast, I cannot run from.
The clock is ticking.
It's a quarter to the hour;
The hour to another pain, to another sword.
Why is life necessary?
What has it gained?
What have we gained from it, but hours?
Hours.
I look for a place of peace and happiness,
But I only find confusion and pain.
I want to create a world of freedom and joy.

But the only words I can write are the ones that fill
my head almost every minute of every day;
Words that I dare not speak out loud.
No one will understand.

01/01/99
11:54pm

"Sleepwalking"

No one can say what I need them to say.
No one can make it better.
They think they know me, but they don't.
They don't see me, so how can they know me?
They don't listen to me, so how can they help me?
I spend my days, biding my time.
I spend my nights wishing they were over.
I tried talking to God, but I'm just more confused.
I've read the book but found no comfort in it.
My reality grows bleaker with each turning of the
page.
I'm tired of feeling guilty for who I am.
I've been apologizing since the beginning.
Never quite right, too bad, too harsh, always
saying the wrong thing.
Waiting in the corner to be approved
Looking and waiting for someone to say, "You're
good enough,"
"Everything will be alright."

The words never come, so I keep on sleepwalking.
Moving aimlessly from one place to another.
Groping like a blind man in a strange and empty
room.
I'm looking and searching for the answers,
But now I know I must look inside myself.

1:07am

02/15/13
8:12pm

"Down But I Ain't Out"

Too this
 too that
So Round
 so Fat
Not enough of this
 too much of that
 Long hair
 short hair
 loc'd hair
 straight hair
Too Bad
 it's not fair
 Not short
 not tall
 not enough
 or none at all
Too loud
 too Strong
Time to sing

a new song
Been high
been low
Searching for
the open door
Ran fast
walked slow
Seen it all
too many times before
Looked up
looked down
The answer
was never found
Prayed up
stood fast
Hoped the pain
wouldn't last
Cried out
whispered soft
Held my breath
thought all was lost
Held on
dug deep
Inside the Kitchen
stood the heat
Went around

came back again
Up the road
 found only a dead end
Dodging mines
 I set myself
Faded Dreams
 on the closet shelf
Looked right
 turned left
Stood still
 took another breath
Boxed in
 boxed out
Tried to scream
 but I couldn't shout
Took the Beat
 And heard the count
Now, I'm down
 But I ain't OUT.

01/11/99
11:54pm

"The Next Snow Fall"

I've sat and wondered.
I've sat and hoped.
I've sat and cried.
This couldn't be all of it;
There has to be more than this.
Where are the movie endings of
        Happily ever after?
                The fairytales of tomorrow land?
What is the necessity of life?
        Necessary to do what?
                To become what?
Haven't I seen this before?
Am I reliving a reality of nightmares?
Where have all the dreams gone?
        Are they hidden away in boxes marked
memories?
        Are they stored away in moving bins labeled
wishes?
I want them back.

I want to hang them in the closet,
> pull them out when things get tough.
> bathe in them when the world gets dirty.

I want to take them out and lay them on a bed of
hope

Oh, if I could dream as I did when I was a child.

But the world changed, and I grew tougher.

I used to look for rainbows,

But the clouds rolled in.

I thought I'd dance in the fresh rains of spring

and let the brightness of the summer sun

wash over me.

But lightening filled the skies

And the summer sun is now the bitter cold of
winter.

I tried to open my mouth to its snowflakes,

But received the cutting winds of a blizzard.

So I stand here,
> Wet, and frozen
>> waiting for the next snow fall.

01/28/01
7:23pm

"Moments"

Moments happen
Brief and fragile
 Time moving
 Time standing still
Not realizing until it's gone
If only we could go back.
If we could capture it in our hands,
 Holding it like a cherished treasure.
In a moment, we are changed
In a moment life is given and taken away
We gather our moments in our minds,
 picking and choosing,
 sorting and collecting,
 reliving, time and again,
We, ourselves, are but moments;
 A collection of moments
 Defining who we are.
In a moment, we love and are loved.
And in a moment, we are memories in
Someone else's collection.

Every Day I Have the Blues

We're Marchin to Zion...

01/16/01
12:17am

(Note: This poem was written the day before I
gave birth to my Son, Jonah.)

"My Jonah"

To love you
　　is to be near you.
To hold you
　　is to experience heaven.
To know sweet peace
　　is to watch you lay restfully in your cradle.
I am moved by your presence
　　and I am in awe of your creation.
You are the sweetest breath of air,
　　and I breathe you in
　　　　as you become my life.
Holding your hand
　　and seeing the generations
　　　　radiating in your eyes.
I am filled with emotions I cannot speak.
　　You are my tomorrows,
　　　　my answered prayers.

You are my love,

my life,
        my forever,
                my Jonah.

1:00am

01/16/00
10:52pm

"One Great Moment in Time"

It surrounds me at night
as I lay awake,
        crying over wishes
        and what never was.
I think of a time of possibilities
        interwoven in hope.
A time when the sun was bright
and my thoughts were of tomorrow.
        A dream seemed a touch away
        and the word, impossible,
        a foreign tongue.
Youth made me optimistic.
Now, I am realistic,
        staring at an empty cup.
My bed has become my thinking post,
        reflecting on "if onlys"
        And "if could'evs."
I close my eyes to make believe,
and I open them to what is.

I look toward the east,
      but I see no new horizons.
I listen for a new song,
      but I hear no instruments.
I pray for a moment,
      one beautiful moment,
            suspended and powerful.
      One great moment in time,
            gone but yet remembered.

04/27/99
10:47pm

"Waiting"

The day begins in the midst of the night.
Slowly, the hand circles round.
I bend my ear to listen to the sound of a new
beginning,
but there is only silence.
The night is filled with dread and uneasiness.
Fear seems to find me fast.
I hope for sleep, but it comes slowly.
My mind is a projector
as each worry acts out it's familiar scene.
The nights are long.
The mornings are quick.
and I wait for the promise of yesterday,
cradled in a dream for the future.
I wait for the dream fulfilled,
a promise honored.
I wait and I grow increasingly tired.
How long must I stand with my nose
pressed to the window-pane of life?
I am anxious to bring the future to the present

and make the present the past.
But my today is long and the hour hand moves
slowly
And I remain waiting.

12:10am

01/29/99

"What's the Word?"

What happens when the one you need doesn't
deliver?
Who failed whom?
Was it me who failed you?
    Myself?
But they said you could not fail.
You said, let there be,
And I tried.
You said, I will,
So I waited.
You said, ask
And I said, may I?
    Can I?
        Would you please?
I heard the voice crying in the wind
And I answered it with my heart.
You said, come,
And I took a step.
You said, seek,
But I have not found.
Where is my help?

My Salvation?
Who's standing at whose door knocking?
You said drink,
I drank, and yet I thirst.
I bow before you in the sunrise of the day
 Knees bent,
   back broken,
     heart aching.
I rise to my feet,
  still broken,
   still bent.
I read, but the words are of no consequence.
Where is my hope?
Who can I trust?
Now faith is the substance,
  but the evidence is not seen.
You said as a mustard seed
so I said I believe
  but still I wait.
I searched the book for reasons.
The parables are words of confusion.
Teach and I will learn,
But I grow weary with each turning of the page.
I am in the pit of despair
  and yes, this is hell.
   Hell, like I've never known,

yet, I know there is something worse, and so, I
run.
I run hard,
I run fast.
But the conveyor belt continues to turn
and I am still running.
I hear my voice crying deep from within my soul.
Lord, have mercy.
But the words lay in the pit like a body released
from life.
Is there mercy in life or in death?
I am struggling,
needing to find peace
Gather the Elders,
the wise men
and the prophets.
Who can understand my words?
Who can hear my cries?
Who can read the book and tell me what it says?
I am still.
I am holding my breath.
What's the word?
I heard of a man;

he's got the word.
What's the word?
He ain't tellin'.
Lord, have mercy.

8:25pm

01/20/99
10:27pm

"Confusion"

What I think,
      I don't know.
What I know
      leaves me only confused.
Confused of this,
      Confused of that.
The look,
      the sound,
            the smell of life.
The dream,
      The fantasy,
            the realness of life.
Yesterday,
      Today,
            Tomorrow,
This world,
      That planet,
            a universe.
I listen for a sound,
         a word;

Something that makes sense,
        A verse
                to make the monotony seem
profound
        And meaningful.
Life,
    the game,
            the reality of pain.
What?
        I hear myself saying a word.
Are you talking to me?
Did I hear you call my name?
What?
        No, I didn't think so.
Confusion.
        Life.
By whose definition?
Did someone say something?
Did you call my name?
What's the word?
You know the word?
        You told me last night
But I think I was sleep.
Did I hear the word?
What did you say softly
        In the loudness of night?

The word, in the thickness of loneliness.
    The agony of time.
I thought I heard something…
    Confusion.

11:50pm

06/23/99
10:59pm

"Motionless Feet"

Life,
     an energy of massive proportions
     fueling the earth with
          movement and sound,
leading to the fulfillment of song.
     A musical of instruments
     reaching life's crescendo,
     crashing to the depths
          of silence.
I've heard the melodies
     of hope.
I've read the lyrics
     of possibilities,
and I have snapped my fingers
     to the rhythms of yesterday.
The songs were sweeter then,
the voices much more in harmony.
I danced to the joy of the music.
I hummed its familiar tune.
I've played the instruments of love

and gazed into the brightness
of sorrow.
I've breathed its clarity
and I've mourned its bitter notes.
The piano
is now out of tune.
The pitch is not quite right.
What used to be music
is now the crackling sounds
of an old phonograph,
and my feet remain
Motionless.

12:30am

02/01/99
10:00pm

"**Broken** Reflection"

Who is this stranger who stands before me,
    so familiar,
        yet, unrecognizable?
I know the face.
    I've seen those eyes before.
    so familiar
        a scent,
            a touch.
I know I've seen that face before.
I've heard that voice,
    crying loud in the silence of the night,
        sobbing deep from within the soul.
A fuse had been lit.
The fire burning inside.
    A scream,
    "GET ME OUT OF HERE!"
    A look.
    The turn of a phrase
        ignites an explosion,

fierce and often regrettable.
A mounting eruption
leaving smoldering shame.
Who is this timely grenade?
I've seen those eyes before.
I know the sound of that voice.
Something is so familiar.
I look and see a broken
reflection.

10:58pm

01/20/99

"Somewhere Between Wishes and Hope"

I am bewildered.
standing here, looking at the brightness of
darkness.
Standing in the shadows of emptiness.
groping in a room of loneliness.
    There is no music.
    There is no sound at all.
      The loudness of nothing,
    the tender breath of despair.
    A moment of gentle hope.
Yesterday
      I could dream.
Yesterday
      I could believe,
But there is no sigh of relief;
      only sweet breaths of anticipation.
Eagerness left with youth
      So willing to dream,
      So ready to hope.
The reality of life is all I have left,
But still, I desire to dream of tomorrow.

But instead, I grieve of today.

> This hour,
> This moment;

But I hear tale of a place
Where dreams bloom all year round.

> Where the sweet smell of success permeates

the air.

> Where it is, I couldn't tell.

How to get there, I don't know,
But I do know, it's across the river of confusion.
Sitting on a mountain of wishes.
Smack in the middle of hope.

12:31am

It's A Family Affair

I Am Seeking for A City

01/28/01
6:03pm

"My Baby Boy"

My Baby boy,
so little and fragile.
So beautiful.
I've traced your face with my eyes a thousand
times.
Your little hands, I've held in mine.
No joy I've ever known
Until that first cry of hello.
Each sound you make
Let's me know I need to be better.
        Protect you,
                Teach you,
                        Raise you,
and for that, I look toward Zion.
You are my reason
and my new beginning.
A flickering flame I can make bright,
Surrounding you with all the love I have.
Teaching you to walk in God's ways.
Look to the Father for strength and guidance.

Through His love and protection
you will grow.
By His mercy your light will shine,
and by His grace, you will find joy everlasting.
You are my blessing from God.
My dove of Peace,
My prayer for the future,
My dream fulfilled.
Your eyes keep me focused
and my path is well-defined.

7:19pm

06/08/01
9:47am

A Poem for "Mommy"
A day before her birthday

Oh, if I could be like You.
Where did you come from?
God must have fashioned you
     with his own hands.
With Mercy,
     we have been blessed to know you.
With Grace,
     He has given us, You.
You are our beginning.
We are trees,
     basking in the fullness of your love.
You are the river of wisdom
     which flows to our roots,
and we stand tall as the oak
     knowing that,
          because of You,
               We Are.

08/04/99
2:01am

"I Love You Still"

I knew you so well;
    Your light,
    Your grace,
    Your warmth,
    Your smell,
        Your walk,
        Your sway,
        The words, you'd say.
I knew it all well;
    Your voice,
    Your tone,
    Not quite a baritone,
        Your face,
        Your brow,
        Your one and only dimple.
You filled my world with joy.
You made it all so simple.
    The touch of your hand.
    Your kiss on my cheek.
    Your smile so wide.

and your big, flat feet.
Tony, I knew you so well.
I loved you then.
　　　I love you still.
In all the world there will never
Be another
Because you will always be
my big brother
and I will always know you so well.

3:47am

03/12/01

"Felicia's Blues"

Don't know why ole man trouble
  been sittin' in my livin' room.
    Been sittin in my livin' room
      causin' my light not to shine.
I've been singin' da blues,
  been singin' da blues two times.
Sho' nuf hard on a 'oman.
  Been askin' da questions.
    Been waitin' on da answers.
  Ain't nobody talkin,'
    so I jus keep listenin'.
Heard dat rainbows don't shine
  on cloudy days.
    Days so long,
      nights so short.
        Days turn into nights,
        todays become
yesterdays
and I'm still sittin' here,
  Singing tomorrow's blues.
Billie say,
  "God bless the chile who's got his own."

I say,
    "God bless the chile to get his own."
Ain't no easy streets marked "life,"
        only unpaved roads leading to possibilities,
            leaving trails of what was.

11:41am

10/11/18
1:59am

"Embodiment of Cool"

When I was younger
I wanted to be around you
      even though you pushed me away.
I thought you were superman,
      able to leap tall buildings in a single bound.
I thought you could solve every problem,
      fix any and everything.
I thought you were brilliant, charismatic, and
suave.
For me, you were the embodiment of Cool.
But as I grew older, the rose-colored glasses
      became spectacles of clarity.
And frightful realities
      became painful memories.
The best of you, was never enough,
      and the worst of you, was way too much.
I wanted to blame you,
      and for a time I did.
But I realized you are a collection of those who
      raised you.

A result of times and experiences that have come
      to define you
And it is because of you
         that I am.

3:21pm

I Never Dreamed You'd Leave

In Summer

I Must Walk My Lonesome Valley...

06/08/01
8:57am

"A Poem for Sugar man"

Through your eyes of discovery,
the world is new.
Through your vision,
life is made fresh.
By your smile,
the colors of the rainbow are vivid,
splashes of possibilities.
Because of your presence,
I have become born again.
Your life is my breath of purpose.
Your breath is my strength to be better.
In you, I have found the hope of my youth.
Because of you, I can dream again.
You are my precious treasure.
My muse.
My light.
My always.
My Ezra.

05/05/99
1:30am

"The Spoken Word of Life"

She is the spoken word of life;
The very definition of the word.
Her eyes are the reflections of the past.
Her words are the rivers of wisdom and
understanding.
Her image is proof of God's power on earth,
though her movement is slow from the passing of
time.
The strength of many lives she holds in her breast.
I am made small in the shadow of her essence.
Yet, because of her, I can reach unreachable
heights.
The moon cannot contain her love,
Nor the sun her warmth.
Heavy is her touch,
Yet tenderness radiates from it.
Her smile is the dawn of new day.
She is my beginning,
      My aspiration,
        My Prayer;

For she is my MOTHER,
And through her,
       I am made new once again.

2:15am

01/17/99
10:27pm

"323 Days"

What is this world without the sunlight,
    Without the music;
The music that filled my soul with complete
    abandonment?
I was free to be me
    And not have to apologize.
I could hear my own voice
    Trembling in laughter,
        Trying to catch my breath.
When my cup was empty,
    Your smile filled it with hope.
You were my hope,
        My reasoning,
            My voice of "ok."
You laughed and the whole world seemed
    conquerable.
I stare into today and there is no sunlight.
    The raindrops are bigger,
        Falling faster.
The air is harder to breathe;

It is filled with thick clouds of loneliness
And I am choking.
An hour is a day
And a day is an eternity.
The laughter is gone.
Yesterday is my place of serenity,
My joy.
I looked at the clock,
It is 10:00 p.m.
323 days since you left.
323 days without the sun,
Without my friend,
Without my brother;
323 days.

07/27/01
11:01pm

"Faded Memories Stained with Tears"

If I could see your face once again,
See your smile and breathe you in
I would know true happiness.
I am but half of what I used to be,
Before you were taken away.
I am the shadow in your essence left behind,
Wishing for a taste of yesterday.
We were two souls lifting each other higher,
Dancing in one another's rhythms.
Now my steps are out of sync.
I am searching for a new beat.
As I sit here thinking of you,
Your scent is in the air.
So I look for you, but there is only a picture,
A vase,
A book on a shelf,
A shirt hanging in the closet.
And I am left with memories,
Faded and stained with tears.

11:56pm

Keep Ya Head Up

O Mary Don't You Weep...

09/22/18
8:28am

"NO VACANCIES"

Hey you,
How you doin'?
Oh, me? I'm good.
I just came to tell you,
it's time for you to go.
Don't look so shocked.
I think you've stayed long enough.
Your stuff?
Oh, don't worry about that,
I've been packing that up for a while.
Yes Lawd, today is your moving day.
See, one day I woke up too tired to be that sick
and tired of You.
So, you've gotta go.
Oh yes, I thought you had me.
I was down.
I was so low, I had to reach up just to touch
bottom.
But one thing you didn't count on

Was me, finding ME.
That's right, I found Myself.
I was broken.
I was bruised.
I needed dusting off,
But the one thing I didn't need
Was YOU.
So, it's time.
You gotta go.
Don't worry, your bags are by the door.
And all the friends you came with;
Doubt, worry, and self-hatred,
They're waiting to leave out with you.
Yes Baby, today is your eviction day.
I'm done.
And you're done taking up residence in my soul.
Cause I found out that I AM GOOD ENOUGH.
That's Right,
I AM GOOD ENOUGH.
Every roll, every bump, every curve.
My thighs, my breasts, my stretch marks.
My lips, my eyes, my hair; from head to toe,
I AM GOOD ENOUGH.
You thought you had me broken.
Yes I was, but not shattered.

It took a long time to recover, but here I am, and you, can hit the door.
You don't have a home here anymore.
Round it up, Insecurity.
You've been served your papers.
I've met some new friends, as a matter of fact, here they come.
Meet strength, the twins: Self-love and Self Respect.
Come on in, faith, and have a seat.
So you see, there's no room for you here anymore.
And on your way out, don't forget to hang this sign on the door,
"NO VACANCIES"

9:02am

11/30/18
11:55am

"Backside of Nothing"

I wake
    Faced down.
I rollover.
    I stumble.
Seven days
    I'm scuffling.
        Trying to get off the back side of
nothing.
I'm counting.
    Adding and dividing.
        Subtracting.
Making meatloaf appear to be crown roast.
    I'm Hustling.
        Trying to get off the back side of
nothing
I'm running.
    I'm stumbling.
I'm tripping and falling.

But I get up.
I fumble.
      Trying to get off the back side of
nothing.
I'm praying.
    I'm crying.
I'm stuttering
    and lying.
Needing to change a dollar into a hundred.
A hundred would get me over the hump;
    Three would make it even.
      Trying to get off the back side of
nothing.
I'm walking fast
    and running slow.
I'm crossing the street.
    I'm jogging.
    I'm Juggling.
I'm searching for the right way to go
    So I can get off the back side of
nothing.
I'm out of breath.
I'm slowing down.
    Leaning to one side.
I stretch out my hand,
    groping,

weaving,
        bobbing.
You know what nothing from nothing leaves.
I turn around.
    I glance back.
I look forward.
    I stand still.
        Still, on the back side of nothing.

04/28/99
12:23am

"Chastisement"

What does one write when there are no words?
There is no beginning,
just a blank sheet of paper.
The emotions I feel are scattered and undefined.
I don't understand this limbo.
The harder I think, the words continue to elude
me.
There is nothing I can do, yet I don't know what to
do.
The feeling of helplessness overtakes me.
And then I grow angry.
Angry, because I do feel helpless;
Helpless to change my circumstances.
Waiting like a child to be taken by the hand and
lead out of this darkness.
I thought I saw a light through this long tunnel,
But as I push forward, I feel the tunnel closing
around me.
I want to yell, but that won't help.
I'm tired of being face down.

I want to turn and breathe again.
I believed in myself once.
I had courage, faith, and determination.
But I have been whittled like a stick.
I have been stripped and left in the nakedness
of self-pity.
I grow tired of my own doubts
And yes, it is night once again.
God, would that it was morning
A reflection of a thousand days past,
Whittled at the tick of a clock.
Is there any mercy for me?
What is the crime for this punishment?
I am drowning in chastisement.

12:46am

10/10/18
12:02pm

"Lifeboat on the Horizon"

What happens when your mind
    becomes your enemy?
When your desires become your foes?
Common sense tells you to walk away,
But something inside won't let go.
You've weighed the balances.
You know the scale is leaning toward the exit,
But something keeps telling you,
    NOT YET.
A thousand voices are screaming,
    This is not right!
They say,
    Love is not selfish;
    It does not ask more of you
    than it is willing to give back.
    Love does not make you feel less.
You've known love.
You've known it, intimately and personally.
You've felt its tenderness and strength.

You've been enraptured in its joy and hope.
>Willing you to be more than you thought
>you could be.
>Causing you to look to the future and make
>plans for tomorrow.

But this, this is empty and hollow.
It is not lifting, but plunging.
It is not willing, but dragging.
It washes over you like a tidal wave of illusion.
And some tidal waves are not waves,
>But TSUNAMIS;
>>Destructive,
>>>Threatening
>>>>And Life-destroying.

When will you hear the warning signals
>Telling you to evacuate the premises?
When will you hear the sirens?
They are not sweet melodies
>beckoning you forward,
They are warning bells
>telling you to retreat and take cover.
Stop holding on to driftwood
When there is a life boat on the horizon.
12:57pm

10/06/02
9:00pm

"Keep Running"

My best laid plans
Were interrupted by life
As I walked down the street of possibilities.
I took the detour of uncertainty.
I looked up
And I was standing at the door of
I never would have believed.
What do you do when you're running
to catch up to your own life?
YOU KEEP RUNNING.

03/13/01
4:54pm

"He Who Controls It"

Standing outside
    looking in,
wanting to scream,
    unable to whisper.
I hear my name,
    but I'm unable to answer.
I see my shadow,
    but I'm unable to touch it.
I'm reaching out my hand,
    trying to get a piece of control.
    Control what seems to be out of control.
There are no wise men,
    no soothsayers,
    no calming words.
Where are the Prophets,
    the Pharisees?
They have all gone astray,
    blinded by greed and ambition.
Who does life belong to?

She who lives it,
or He who controls it?
I am a participant
feeling like an observer.
I am the starting line-up
watching from the sidelines.
I am the main actor
playing the supporting role.
I am the puppeteer
feeling like the puppet.
Who does life belong to?
She who lives it,
or he who controls it?

02/12/01
9:46am

"Sista's Serenade"

Girl,
what you been doin'?
You been livin'
    and life done caught you off guard.
I heard you been talkin',
    talkin' to da preacher man,
    talkin' to yo friend down da hall.
You even been talkin to dat ole man on da corna.
Did dey tell you anything you wanna hear?
What you wanna know, sista girl?
    Will the snow fall tomorrow?
What you wanna know?
    How the rain fell in Spain?
Listen girl,
    ain't no streets called easy.
    No sun-drenched paths leading to
    brighter tomorrows.
Ain't no prince charmin's
    coming down no yellow brick roads.
It just AIN'T.

You gotta get yo head togetha.
    Today ain't yesterday,
    and yesterday ain't tomorrow.
We livin' for TODAY,
    And TODAY is all it IS.
You reflect back too long,
You find yoself lost in what WAS.
Ain't no, wish I could 'eves
    or if onlys.
All it is,
    is what it is.
        You dig what I'm sayin'?

10:34am

09/22/18
6:00pm

"Rise Up"

Rise up.
Shake the dust off your shoes.
Rise up
And stop singing the blues.
Rise up
And change that old song.
Rise up.
You've been singing that one way too long.
Rise up
And like Janet, take control.
Rise up
And be good to your soul.
Rise up
And wash your face.
Rise up
Because the bottom is not your place.
Get on up, girl.
Do your dance.
Never be afraid
to take your chance.

Stand on up, girl.
Stand on your feet.
Don't let nobody tell you, to take a seat.
Scream out.
Let the world hear your voice.
Tell the man no, it is my choice.
Stand up, girl.
Scream and shout.
Let the world know what we're about.
Tell them all,
Both great and small.
Don't sit down and don't apologize.
Rise up, girl and tell the world,
Y'all better recognize.

7:08pm

02/17/13
8:53pm

"A Beginning"

A look
A smile
A sweet "Hello"
A touch
A shift
A nod
A blush
A frown
A stutter
A mis-spoken word
A correction
A nervous laugh
A compliment
A flutter
Licked lips
An awkward silence
A turn
A stop
An exchange

An exit
A Beginning.

9:40pm

02/14/00
3:01am

"OUR JOURNEY BEGINS"

(A Poem for Chyrel & Micheal
On their wedding day)

Hey there, brotha man.
Black man,
Hebrew man,
My man.
Can I just rap to you for a minute?
I mean,
Thin line
So fine.
Can I have a piece of yo' time?
It's all about the real.
I mean,
Tell me what you know.
I'll tell you what I know
And together, you and me,
We can just flow.
You know what I'm sayin'?
In the light of your eyes
I see the fathers;

I'm talkin', Abraham, Isaac, and Jacob.
Hey man,
Can I be yo Rachel?
Can we do this thang?
Take it back to the beginning?
In the essence of yo smile
I see the creation.
Feeling your stimulation.
You digging my vibration?
Check this out Black man,
You and I
Joining as one,
Prayin' as one,
Movin' as one.
Two separate entities,
But one mind.
Lovin' and holdin'
One another,
Uplifting each other.
Until the ancient of days come
And make us all one.
You dig my flow?
You see where I'm comin' from?
I'm talkin to you.
Long and lean,
Loc'd up tight,

Lookin' so right.
Let's dance to the beat of this rhythm
Called life.
I take yo hand,
You take mine
And together we move
Into the end of time.
We start our journey
In the sixth month,
On the twenty-fifth day
In this year
Two-thou.
You takin' me,
Me takin' you
And together we vow
These vows.
Sharin' our love
Before GOD,
Family,
And Friends.
In oneness
today.
Our journey begins.

8:53am

Dark N' Lovely

On *My Journey to Mount Zion...*

09/24/18
3:17pm

"Always Look Towards Zion"

Jonah,
You are 17 years old now
And I have had the privilege of spending all that
time with you.
    Talking with you,
        Teaching and guiding you
            and yes, learning from you.
I used to wonder what my life's purpose was,
But you came and all became clear.
That's what you have given me;
    Clarity in a world of uncertainty and
confusion.
I look at you becoming a man,
    and I look back on that winter day
    and your first cry of hello.
I am filled with all you have given me:
    Pride,
        Joy,
            Love and Hope.

As you are preparing to take your place in the
world,
    and no matter where you go
    or how far you go,
I hope you always know,
    I AM your anchor.
No matter how the wind blows,
I am here to hold you down.
To steady you in place
when the waves of life pull you
    here and there.
Keep your eyes on the horizon, son,
And always, always look towards Zion.

3:28pm

05/09/99
12:20am

"BLACK LIKE ME"

BLACK
    LIKE WHO
BLACK
    LIKE ME
BLACK
    LIKE YOU
        BLACK
SO BLACK YOU'RE ALMOST BLUE
    DARK CHOCOLATE
    MILK CHOCOLATE
    EVEN WHITE CHOCOLATE
        BLACK
BLACK
    LIKE THE NIGHT
    SMOOTH AND RIGHT
BLACK
    LIKE THE DARK SIDE OF THE MOON
        RYTHMICALLY
            EROCTICALLY
BLACK

LIKE A MILES DAVIS TUNE
SO BLACK
YOU'RE ALMOST PURPLE
MYSTICAL
MAGICAL
DOWN RIGHT MYTHOLOGICAL
LIKE PHARAOH INSIDE HIS TOMB
BLACK
BLACK
LIKE WHO
BLACK
LIKE ME

2:05am

10/30/18
2:30pm

"Why You Hate Me"

Why you hate me?

You hate me because I walk and I sway to the rhythm of my own greatness, which God gave me from the beginning of time.

You hate me because when I talk, I flow like the waters of the Egyptian Nile.

You hate me because my eyes glow with the history of an entire nation of priests and kings.

You hate me because my rich, dark chocolate skin radiates and reflects the sun, which lights the whole earth.

You hate me because my lips are full and soft with a sensuous curve, speaking the proverbs of Solomon.

You hate me because my kinky, soft hair crowns my head like my father Adam and my mother Eve.

You hate me because my body was carved by the master sculptor, Jehovah.

You hate me because you spend your days and nights thinking of new ways to hold me down, but still I rise, soaring higher and higher.

You hate me because, like King David, I excel at your own tests of strength.
I run, I jump, I climb, I catch, I throw, and I beat you at your own game.

You hate me because I won't let you define me, and tell me who and what you want me to be, because you're afraid of who I really am.

You hate me because You want to be ME.

3:00p.m.

09/23/18
7:39am

"Civil Rights Lost"

So much going on in the world today.
So much to see.
So much to say.
Right up the street
And outside my front door.
Love don't live in the hood no more.
A boom, a bang, a very loud pow
Leaves many mothers asking why and how.
Why is this happening?
How can we stop it?
While the politicians just try and drop it.
Who you gonna vote for, this coming fall?
While many ask the question
Should we even vote at all?
The faces keep changing.
The names rearranging.
Everybody's promising
And everybody's lying.
While our young, black brothers keep on dying.
We've marched.

We've sang.
We thought we over-came.
We've sat down.
We've stood up.
We're tired of drinking from this full cup.
We've pounded our fists
And demanded justice,
But the only people going through this, is just us.
Like Marvin said, it makes you wanna holler,
Raise your fist and scream Black Power
But we've done all that before.
And we're still pounding on the door.
From the dreaming of dreams
To the urgency of now,
Our civil rights remain lost somehow.

8:41am

10/30/18
9:00am

"Homage to the Brotha's"

Excuse me brotha,
    I mean, King.
Rich Chocolate, high yellow, creamy caramel
brotha.
Can I just lay this out to you for a minute?
Tall and lean,
Thick and Stacked,
Short and pumped,
My brotha, you are all that.
You are the beginning of life and I bask in the
glory of you.
You are strength and power
and I want to sit at your side and absorb your
greatness.
Your eyes are smoldering, tender coals of sexy
and when you pimp and walk, I swear I hear a
Curtis Mayfield tune.
You are a perfect imperfection
and the very definition of right.
Your mouth is the tongue of experience

and I learn at your altar of wisdom.
You are cool and suave, intelligent and talented
and I shine brighter in your presence.
You are the foundation
and I stand on your shoulders, reaching for the
wholeness of family.
You sing your blues.
You play your jazz.
You rap your hip-hop
and I sway my hips to your beat.
I dig who you are and what you're about
and I think it's time someone said it.

9:30am

11/04/99
4:40pm

"A Poem for Michelle & Jonathan"

Brotha Man,
Brotha Man,
     Let me bend yo ear.
Been look'n
And I been took'n.
     But now you're finally here.
I was lost
And I paid the cost,
     But the Lawd had mercy on me.
I hit my knees,
     Said Lawd please, please.
Looked up and yo smile set me free.
I give you my hand
     And now here we stand,
In front of God, Family and Friends
     To vow these vows.
     To walk as one
        Until our journey ends.
Brotha Man,
Brotha Man,

Da Lawd,
     He knew the plan.
He knew from the start
     You'd have my heart.
And now, our life begins
This fall day.
     This 4th of November
We will always cherish and remember,
For without sadness or gloom
     We jumped da broom
To live a fairy-tale
     happily ever after.

12/08/99
12:07am

"People Lost"

Who is dees people
walkin' round
    with their pantses hangin' down,
        strange hair do's
        and jive talk?
I hear tell
    dey don't know who dey is.
Dey call themselves
    African
        American,
but the Africans say
    it ain't so.
What yo name is?
    YOU
        who don't answer to nobody,
        but everybody is listening.
    YOU
        who ain't got no name,
        but known by many names.

White folk call you
    NIGGER,
then they got sophisticated
    And called you
    NEGROES.
What yo name is?
    YOU
            with yo kinky hair,
            straight hair,
                weaved hair,
                    curly hair,
                        no hair.
Someone said you was black,
    but dat's just a color.
Another said you were Afro-American,
    but last I heard, Afro
        ain't nothin' but a hair-do.
How come you da only one's
    don't know who you is?
    IRISH,
        SPANISH,
            GREEK,
                ITALIAN.
What you is,
    BLACK man?
        GOD only knows.

Jacob lay hold
But nobody knows.
Heard you was lost for forty years.
Kings and Queens
begat your name,
Then time stood still
and you lost again.
Kicked out,
Sold and bought.
Whipped and
chained
And you forgot your name.
Who you is,
Mr. and Mrs. Black?
wit yo cottin pickin' hands;
singin' yo plantation blues,
eaten yo hot sauce
and chittlins.
Yeah,
I saw you marchin in da streets
carry'in' yo signs,
sittin at dem lunch counters,
talkin' bout we shall
over-come.
I got yo BLACK POWER,
BLACK IS BEAUTIFUL,

BLACK IS BACK,
IT'S A BLACK
THANG.
Yeah,
You thought you finally arrived,
EMANCIPATED,
SEGREGATED,
INTERGRATED,
Now EDUCATED.
Look,
there you is in yo Givonche suits,
driving yo Mercedes Benz
working on Wall Street
living in Manhattan.
Oh yeah,
that affirmative action is som'n else,
But the Uncle in the Supreme house
said
Y'all don't need dat no mo.
Now,
you're lookin' fo a friend,
but most of dem are in da county
do'in' ten
Man,
dees people shole are strange,
layin' hold to someone else's name.

Now,
>I hear tell, dere is a book;
It's sittin on yo shelf,
>dust it off and take a look.
Unstick da pages
>and walk through da ages;
One by one
>until you're done.
Pay ATTENTION
>and read real slow.
Break it down
>and den y'all know.
Now dat yo've come to da end,
>I'll ask my question once again,
WHAT YO NAME IS
>AND WHO YOU BE?
You closed THE BOOK
>And smile at me.

12/08/99
2:15am

05/05/99
8:25am

"Words Etched in Stone"

A people without a name
who lost their fame
    Judged to shame
They sold out
without a fight
but reaped the pain, both day and night.
They sold their souls,
but not for gold.
They lost their minds,
but not with wine.
They said all you say,
    we will do.
but they turned aside
before the night was through.
The words were sure,
    written in stone
but their hearts were hard,
    couldn't leave sin alone.
Now their backs are broken

and all hope is lost.
I know they wish now
    they would have counted the cost.
Was it worth all the beatings the massa's gave,
    changing their names from king and queen
    to that of slaves?
Seeing their brothers being lynched in trees,
    they searched for their God
upon their knees.
They've been gone too long,
    they don't know where to look,
but then they heard a voice say,
    Read the book.
They turned the page,
    it said face the east.
Women, cover your heads
    as we all pray for peace.
The Lord said, you are all mine;
    I haven't forgotten you,
but will you keep the law
    that I have commanded you?
So you don't bare false witness
    and you don't kill.
You honor your mother and father
    and you don't steal.
You remember the Sabbath Day

to keep it Holy.
Don't Serve other Gods;
Give the God of Israel all the Glory.
Graven images you don't make.
Commit adultery,
in hell you'll wake.
In vain,
don't you take His name.
For eternal life
Better not covet your neighbor's wife.
This is the law you must understand.
God wrote it down for every man.
The story I have told is both tried and true
of the people who are known as the real
Hebrew.

01:20am

03/23/99
11:27am

"Finally Heard the Sound"

What is this rockin', lyrical rhythm thumping
through my body,
making me want to shout;
Shout with song, shout with praise.
Moving my body in harmonious curves to the
beat;
The beat of rhythmic, rhymes, tuned with glorious
melodies of possibilities.
What is this sound ringing in my ears,
causes me to leap and gyrate across the floor with
an energy so pure?
It must be from heaven.
The sound, first soft and steady,
Now loud and strong,
causing me to react in quick steps and movement.
I hear my voice laughing.
I hear a soft sigh of relief.
I'm clapping and snapping my fingers.
I pass and look into a mirror,
seeing myself, carrying on with such joy,

and I realize that the melody I'm humming,
The thumping beat my feet can't stay still for
Is the sound, y'all.
The sound!
It's hope, y'all;
The sound of sweet hope.
Thank GOD I finally heard the sound!

11:37am

10/05/99
1:55pm

"Three Times You Called"

What do you say to the man
  when you hit your knees?
Three times I heard you call,
  four times.
    Have Mercy
You got troubles, man;
   they come visiting you at night
     when you're all alone in your bed.
You've been crying, man
   someone done broke your heart?
What do you say to the man
   when you hit your knees?
I heard you cry
   three times,
     four.
What be on your mind
   when the moon's shining bright?
What stops your heart
   and causes you to shake?
The wind don't blow between

four walls
　　　　but I saw you shake.
Did I hear you sighing, man?
　　　　I thought I heard you sigh.
Old man trouble been dancing around
　　　　in your head.
The only rhythm you hear
　　　　is the sound of your own breath
　　　　　　as it strains to catch the beat.
What's been going on in your life?
The treadmill don't stop turning
　　　　and you just keep on running.
What you say to the MAN
　　　　when you hit your knees?
　　　　I heard you call his name
　　　　　　three times,
　　　　　　　　four.
LORD HAVE MERCY!

10/06/99
4:30pm

02/09/99
9:12am

"Cool Cat Joe"

Who dat
    Cool cat?
Dat's Cool Cat Joe.
Been here,
    done dat.
He done seen dat befo.
    Fakin' and shakin'
    Lyin' and spyin'.
Dat joe is always on the go;
    Slippin' and slidin'
    Jerkin' and flirtin'.
Yeah,
    He hit dat a week ago.
Mommy for Polly,
Niecy and Triecy
    And ole Joe
        Is out da do'
Who dat?
    cool cat?

He ain't got time for you
No mo'.

10/05/99
1:26am

"Shadows of Loneliness"

My mind falls on you,
    Though we've never met.
Your reality is a prayer
    I hold in a quiet place.
I think of the day,
    The time,
        The place.
What will I be wearing?
Will I know you when I see you?
Will you know me?
Will our hearts cry out to one another
    from a place where only you and I have
        dreamed?
Will we recognize one another's voice,
    singing a song only you and I have danced
to?
You have haunted me and I have looked for you
    through the shadows of loneliness.
I have reached for you.

though, I could not feel you,
I have held you close
    like a life jacket in the waters of despair.
You have become my oxygen
    And I breathe you in like the air of hope.

2:17am

Where Peaceful Waters Flow

Stand Still Jordan...

05/05/99
12:26am

"Mystified"

I want to fall deep into your strength,

hearing nothing but the loudness of silence.

Discover your beauty and your hidden treasures.

Your blue is like the softness of clouds spreading

to infinity.

The power which you possess,

makes me feel as if God is near.

The scent of you is that of a fresh, new beginning.

You cradle me like a rocking baby.

You are tender, yet your power is lethal.

Your beauty is comparable to liquid crystal,

translucent with all the colors of the rainbow.

To hear you is to thirst.

To feel you is to be baptized and be born anew.

To know you is to discover a world unknown.

You have my respect and fear.

Your mass and depths invite exploration.

How far do you reach?
How deep can I sink?
What secrets do you hold?
You are a mystery
And I am mystified.

12:47am

02/14/13
1:29pm

"Possibility of Maybe"

I thought about tomorrow;
The possibilities of maybe,
The hope of what if.
What if the unreachable
Could be reached?
What if, What if was
And the dreams of tomorrow were today's
realities?
What if they poured over us like April rain?
Would it free us from the mistakes of yesterday?
Would yesterday rinse away,
Or would it leave the residue of regret?
We say in our hearts and minds, if only,
It becomes our silent prayer.
If only our desires were enough to make it so,
But our desires are only shadows in the clouds of
what is today.

1:57pm

05/12/99
12:41am

"Imagine"

Imagine, if you will,
    a garden.
Full of God's creation.
    so vast,
        so wide.
You revel in its magnificence.
In the midst of the garden
    Was me.
Would I be perfect,
    as perfect as the rising sun?
Sweet,
    as the gentle breeze of spring?
Could I bring the rain
    which sustains every living thing?
Could I be like the stars
    which shine by night?
        Or could I glow like the mysterious
           moon?
Imagine, if you will,

an ocean
so vast and wide,
so clear blue, the fish
actually look back at you.
And in the midst of the ocean
was me.
Would I be as perfect
as the rising of the tide?
Could I reflect the beauty of life
contained within?
Could I hold the romance of ships
that have sailed the stormy waters?
Imagine, if you will,
a house;
an old house
with painted walls
and cluttered shelves.
In the midst of the house
stood me.
Could I tell the stories
of old?
Could I weather the elements
of time?
Could I protect the precious
treasures I held?
Imagine, if you will,

                    a house
                         with a garden
                              near an ocean
and ME, standing in the midst of it.
                         Yes, I can Imagine.

1:56am

05/21/99
2:02pm

"The Window Seat"

I sit in the window seat,
      trying to define myself.
My mind is cluttered,
      yet the page remains empty.
Self-definition can almost be
      too revealing.
Sometimes the mind accepts,
      sometimes it rejects,
and oftentimes,
      it just disregards.
Like most,
      I am defined by experience,
         people,
            places.
I am a combination of personalities
      and realities.
I am a searcher,
      searching for the necessity of life.
I am a student of WHY.
I am a product of the past,

a wonderer of the present
and a dreamer of the future.
I am an infusion of knowledge,
emotion and strength.
I am moved by the creation around me,
empowered by those who came before me.
I am less than God,
created to be more than man.
I am a reaper of harvests
and sower of seeds.
I am worn,
but determined.
I am limp,
but still rising.
I am the face of one
but the reflection of a thousand generations
and yet, I am still being defined.

4:14pm

07/10/01
3:36pm

"Still We Move"

We move in this world
    circling,
        weaving,
            never touching.
Seeing
    and being seen,
        but not knowing.
Speaking politely.
        "Hello."
Smiling.
    "How are you?"
Joking and laughing,
    but we pass one another
        not knowing.
We look back.
    A pause.
        We think.
            We move on.
A thought lingers;
    We stop.

We move on,
familiar
but strange.
And still, we move on
without knowing.

04:13pm

01/16/00
11:00pm

"Time"

There are no new revelations.
There are no great resolutions;
Just the passage of time.
There are no great expectations.
No soul-searching reflection;
Just the passage of time.
Time for today.
Waiting for tomorrow
To become yesterday
Time…
Time to start.
Time to be.
Time to end.
Right now.
This day.
This hour.
This minute.

What was.

What is.

What will be.

TIME.

11:47pm

04/14/99
12:12am

"We Became One"

I thought I heard you whisper my name.
Softly, I heard you cry.
A tear fell from your eye.
Softly, I brushed it away.
The day began when I looked into your eyes.
Softly, I gazed into your eyes.
The sound of your voice, low in a tremble as you
spoke.
Softly, trembling, I answered you back.
The sun rose over your body,
Illuminating your rich, brown tones.
Shining as you lay like a new copper penny.
Softly, I stare.
The room is full of your scent.
Softly, I breathe you in.
I want to wrap up in the safeness of you.
Softly, I reached.
I want to tell you the things that are often on my
mind.
Softly, I spoke your name.

You said the word love.
Softly, I move toward you.
You embraced me in your arms.
Softly, I kissed your lips.
Softly, I trembled inside.
Softly, we became one.

12:25am

03/16/01
3:30pm

"Peace"

Peace
> is the sound of the lake splashing against the
> rocks.
Peace
> is the view of the sun as it paints the
horizon.
Peace
> is an open field of fresh spring flowers.
Peace
> is the dawn and the rising of the moon.
Peace
> is the morning dew on the petal of a yellow
> rose.
Peace
> is looking into the loving eyes of a mother.
Peace
> is a sleeping baby,
> > a symphony of violins,

the sweet perfume of nature,

                    the pure sound of

forgiveness.

1:52am

07/15/01
10:16am

"Reflections of Time"

Smiles become sun-drenched memories
in frames standing still on a shelf.
We live our today's, like never-endings.
As though tomorrows were paychecks
already cashed.
Our lives move quickly through the years
and we are halted by the reflections of time.

10:46am

ⅅ

That's All.

Author's Note:

Words are powerful. They can be uplifting, and comforting. Words allow us to really see ourselves. It's because of them we feel. Black Slaves used to sing the words, known as Negro spirituals. These spirituals are the subtitles of the beginning of each chapter within our book. Slaves sang these songs to express the pain and stain of slavery when they could not read or write.

Words validate our pain and provide healing once released into the universe. Writing has been a source of healing. It's my hope that these poems serve as healing for our readers. When your feelings are validated you know you're not alone. You can survive the current storm in your life.

Different Sides of the Same Coin is an honest record and time stamp of moments lived, one mass collection of words. Spoken and sometimes not spoken at all. This book is a celebration of sisterhood. We are unashamed of all that we are.

Our story is told in the rich, soulful, textures of black speech patterns. This was on purpose.

Another intentioned nuance of this work is our inclusion of dates at the time our poems were written. We wanted our readers to know that words withstand the passage of time. Years go by but words remain.

They withstand the test of time. Words surpass life, love, and loss. Whether written, spoken or sung may you find healing and comfort in this collection of poems.

Psalm 118:23-This is the Lord's doing; it is marvelous in our eyes.

CPSIA information can be obtained
at www.ICGtesting.com
Printed in the USA
LVHW032050081019
633405LV00002BA/474/P

9 781723 998348